Concerto in D minor
for Violin and String Orchestra

FELIX MENDELSSOHN (1809-1847)
Edited by YEHUDI MENUHIN

Viola

I

Edition Peters 6070a-VLA

FELIX MENDELSSOHN BARTHOLDY

CONCERTO

for Violin and String Orchestra / für Violine und Streichorchester

D minor / d-Moll
MWV O3

First Edition by / Erstausgabe von
Jehudi Menuhin

Viola

EDITION PETERS

LEIPZIG · LONDON · NEW YORK

Attacca subito

III

Allegro

ISMN 979-0-3007-0752-5

9 790300 707525